CW00516164

A Com
Guide to Autism

How to Connect with Your Autistic Child

Written By

Daniel Faber

Please note the information contained within this document is for educational and entertainment purposes only. All effort has been executed to present accurate, up to date, reliable, complete information. No warranties of any kind are declared or implied. Readers acknowledge that the author is not engaging in the rendering of legal, financial, medical or professional advice. The content within this book has been derived from various sources. Please consult a licensed professional before attempting any techniques outlined in this book.

By reading this document, the reader agrees that under no circumstances is the author responsible for any losses, direct or indirect, that are incurred as a result of the use of information contained within this document, including, but not limited to, errors, omissions, or inaccuracies.

TABLE OF CONTENTS

INTRODUCTION

In this twenty-first century, we have access to so much information, yet we know so little. Anything you wanted to know is literally one search engine click away, and still, millions of people judge and give bad advice regarding autism. In this book, we will explore the topic in detail and look at parenting an autistic child from many perspectives. The job of parenting is difficult already, and getting bad advice only makes it more so. In exploring the topic in general, we will examine what the condition is, as well as take a brief look at some of the things that this book is and what it isn't.

What is autism?

Autism Spectrum Disorder, popularly known as ASD, refers to a wide range of communicative conditions that impairs a person's ability to develop and use social and communicative skills. It is characterized by repetitive behavior, underdeveloped social skills, and poor verbal and non-verbal communicative skills.

People with autism see the world a little bit differently than we do. They are immensely curious, bright, fun, and stimulating, and they are some of the most delightful people you'll ever have the chance of talking to.

What this book is all about?

This book does not recount the grueling details of parenting a child with impaired social skills; it focuses on how beautiful and different people with ASD are instead. In this book, we talk about what it feels like to parent a child with ASD, what to expect, and how it's not so different from parenting a regular child and how it is different.

We also try to dispel all popular myths about people with ASD. We address and consciously try to answer some bigger questions and fears people have about raising autistic children.

Questions like "How much is it going to cost me" and "how are they going to survive without me?" are answered in this book in great detail. This book was written to give a realistic representation of what it means to raise an autistic child.

What this book is not?

It's not ammunition small-minded people can use to justify their prejudice or resentment for people that are different. This was written to help parents, families, and friends who are having a hard time adjusting to their new realities. This book is not a cautionary tale meant to dissuade all parents thinking about raising an autistic child. This is also not a book that psychoanalyzes autistic children and pretends to know what they feel and personally experience.

This book was written to close the gap between those who really understand what it means to have a friend, child, or family member with autism and those that don't. It covers everything parents should know about their children and dealing with their realities. Hopefully, it will also help people who know nothing about autism understand how similar people with autism and people without autism really are.

A Complete Guide to Autism:

How to Connect with Your Autistic Child

Chapter One

TODDLER PARENTING OVERVIEW

Being a parent, anyone can figure out what's going on inside your mind. You feel so much love for your child that you often feel like your chest will explode. You're also constantly worried about your child's safety. You want to make sure they are okay at all times. You may even sometimes wish you could control everything in their life. All these feelings are normal and are a known part of being a parent.

What might not be so clear to you, however, is what goes on in the mind of your toddler. With grown adults, you can simply ask them what they are thinking, and sooner or later, they'll tell you. But, figuring out what's going on in a toddler's mind is much more difficult. Coinsider that toddlers' brains work very differently from yours. They are still developing and they are trying to make sense of the world. Also, because they are new to the world, they inteprete things on their own, based on what they know which isn't much. Add these together and you have a thought process that's vastly different from anything you currently have. And unfortunately, you can't know their mind. Or can you?

The developing mind of your toddler

"Why are you biting me for no good reason?" "Why would you want to put that in your mouth?" "It's just water. Why in God's name would you be afraid of water?" Do these questions sound familiar? If they do, it's probably because they are questions you're constantly asking yourself about your toddler. But, before you can answer these questions, you need to have a fundamental understanding of how your toddler's brain works.

One of the reasons you can't understand why your toddler does the things he does is that his reasoning is still developing, He himself is not quite sure he understands why he does the things he does. It is therefore essential that you understand what your child is visualizing and trying to imbibe into himself. These formative years will determine who your toddler turns out to be, and you want to influence as much of it as you can.

The following illustration will give you a general sense of the developments your toddler is experiencing. Between ages 1 and 2, toddlers learn via sensory input. They also feel and visualize objects. Their objective at this point is to learn to react to their immediate environment. At this age, they also develop emotions and feelings like feeding and rocking. They rely on their caretakers to provide not just physical support, but emotional support as well. Their need for emotional support is even more exaggerated when they are stressed.

Moving on, ages 2 to 7 will see your toddler trying to develop imagination and creativity. He will also develop cognitive skills, logic, memory, reasoning, attention, and emotions. These developments make this particular age bracket very important. As your toddler's memory starts to improve, and he'll be able to remember things more actively. He will also develop the ability to think symbolically and comprehend abstract concepts. At this point, your toddler can also think about the past and the future, in some detail.

While all these developments are taking place, your toddler's mind is also prone to influence by external factors. In fact, all of the development is owing to some influence from the outside. For simplicity's sake, we can break it down into three categories: environmental factors, biological factors, and interpersonal relationships.

The environmental factors include things like nutrition and diet, space for exploration, education and access to books, as well as family relationships. When we talk of biological factors, we're referring to things like family and social treatment, the health of the child and family, and most especially the child's sex. Boys and girls develop differently from each other. The interpersonal relationship's influence on the child's development includes things like attachment towards parents and caregivers, the social circle of friends, and of course, parenting styles.

It's obviously impossible for you to control all these factors. People would think you were crazy if you tried to. But, simply understanding their roles can help you adjust how you relate with and care for your toddler.

Why do they do what they do?

As a parent, you understand more than anyone else that toddlers have needs. That is, if the time you've spent with your child since he was born has taught you anything. The answer to why they do what they do is quite simple. They do what they need to do. Just like it's illogical to ask why toddlers eat or sleep, it's almost as illogical to ask why they throw tantrums. Subconsciously, all parents are grateful that there are some things their toddlers do without any prompts or requests. Like breathing for example. However, you have to prompt them for some other things, like eating and sleeping. The fact still remains that toddlers know to do things on their own, and that's a good thing.

Even for psychological actions like emotional expressions and choices, children don't need to be instructed. Consider the following tendencies, for example. The need for survival, love and belonging, power, freedom, and of course, affection. You don't ever need to tell your child to desire these things. Even though there are more psychological and emotional tendencies than these five, they are basic, and they form the building blocks of everything else. In fact, if you look closely at them, you can identify intersection points between your behavior and theirs. These are places where your actions and the reasons behind them match their actions. So, in understanding your toddler's behavior, you have to keep these tendencies in your mind.

Look at crying, for example. Why do toddlers cry? That's quite simple, right? They cry because they are hungry, or frustrated, or tired, or upset, or thirsty, or cranky, or want to play, or want to stop playing. There is a near-infinite amount of reasons why toddlers cry. An analysis of the toddler's environment can give you a very good idea of how they feel and what they want. Granted, the degree of understanding you get will vary based on many factors, including the ones we discussed earlier under developmental factors. However, a simple awareness of the presence of these factors can enhance your understanding of why they do what they do.

To dig a little deeper into understanding the behavior of your toddler, let's examine the four levels of actions in children. There are actions that are either purposeful, effective, responsible, or in line with pre-established rules. So, if your toddler cries for a lollipop, the action is purposeful. But is it effective? That will depend on whether or not you, as a parent, obliges the request. Also, is the action responsible or irresponsible? There are several ways to judge this action, based on the rules you're laying down in your house. But, a generally accepted notion would be this. If the lollipop belongs to someone else, then the action is certainly not responsible. The responsibility of the action is also closely tied to its relation to laid down laws and regulations.

When it's all said and done as a parent, it's important to understand that even though your toddler's actions may not check all of these boxes, the toddler is currently acting according to its best ability. Very often, naughty toddlers don't know they are naughty. They must be reminded.

Setting up toddlers to thrive

If you've raised a toddler before, the chances are that you're already familiar with at least some of the steps in this section. Your whole job as a parent is to set up your toddlers so that they can get enough freedom and knowledge to express themselves and grow properly. For many parents, preparing your child for life, in general, is more of an unconscious effort. You don't really get up one day and say to yourself, "I'm going to make my child thrive, no matter what it takes." You're more likely to say things like, "I want my child to go to a great school and get good grades." But, at the base of it all, you still want your child to have a great life, which is thriving.

We will cover a lot of tips and advice on creating a thriving environment for your toddlers in the following chapters. But while we're here, let's discuss three straight forward ways that you can promote proper development in your child.

First of all, you should not tell them that they can be anything they want to be. This may seem like counter-intuitive advice, but it's actually backed up by research. A research done by the market research agency, C+R research, found out that young people, especially Americans, are not really interested in doing jobs that are geared for the future. They are more interested in things like music, athletics, and video gaming. Telling your kids that they can be anything they want to be maybe sending them down a path of unemployment. You're better off advising them to focus on more future-oriented jobs in sectors like healthcare and construction trades.

Secondly, don't skip eating dinner together. Most parents try to have dinner together, until a certain point when bills and life's pressures force them to progressively take chunks out of family time. The advice to always eat dinner together is also backed by research conducted by a non-profit organization that operates out of Harvard University. It showed that kids who eat with their families at least five days in a week showed lower tendencies of substance abuse than other kids. They also have higher GPAs, more self-esteem and better vocabulary. The link isn't yet understood, but it's there and it's clear.

Lastly, you should enforce a "no-screen" time for your kids. Again, we'll get more into the importance of scheduling in chapter 6, but for now, let's focus on the negative effects of technology screens on children. Research shows that technology screens can cause permanent changes to the brain of a toddler. The word here is alteration, not damage. The American Academy of Pediatrics recommends that kids younger than the age of 18 months shouldn't have any screen time at all, other than video chatting. You certainly can't deprive them of their call time with mommy or daddy.

Self-Regulation & Keys to Success

Emotional self-regulation is something every parent wants for their children. Imagine if your toddler knew when to throw a tantrum and when to behave. If your child knows when to suck on a lollipop and when to leave it be, parenting would be an absolute joy. But, since that has never happened, it's safe to assume it never will, not on its own anyway. You have a large role to play in ensuring that your kids know how to behave.

To approach self-regulation, Scott Bezsylko, the director of the Winston Prep Schools for children with learning differences, has a very important tip. He says that self-regulation should be approached in the same way other skills in the toddler's life are approached. Skills like academic excellence and social well-being. According to him, thinking of emotional self-regulation as a skill to be taught changes the way you see it, and the way your toddler perceives it. The key is to teach them how to approach difficult situations by providing scaffolding. In essence, introducing them to it one step at a time.

As a final example, consider solving difficult mathematics homework. The ideal way to approach it is to build a scaffold, and that includes solving one problem for your child and expecting the child to try the rest. You must remember to always give the child the opportunity to try his hand and make mistakes. As time progresses, continue solving problems and you'll see the performance soar.

We have now reached the end of this chapter. In this chapter, you should have been able to realize that your toddler's brain is slightly different from yours. You should have learned that even though there's a difference in action, the same motivations drive the two of you. At a basic level is the need for survival. As the actions become more complex, so do the motivations. However, they are all built around the same framework. You should have also learned how to set up your child to thrive using evidence-based rules like limited screen time, intentional career advice, and eating dinner as a family. Lastly, we discussed the ways in which you can teach emotional self-regulation in your children.

These are tips mostly geared towards raising children who do not have Autism Spectrum Disorder. In the following chapters, we'll give the condition full attention and give you a step by step guide on how to parent a child with ASD.

Chapter Two

SOCIAL INTERACTION FOR CHILDREN WITH AUTISM

Some of the biggest problems that children with autism experience are, engaging in social interactions, and maintaining relationships. They typically don't process and react to information in ways that you'd expect. Children with autism sometimes find new experiences jarring and uncomfortable, and so, it's important to understand them and teach them to defuse potentially triggering situations.

Social skills are important for all humans because they are survival skills, and every single human needs them to function and thrive. Especially in modern society. Social skills allow you to create and maintain important relationships and participate in community building exercises. They are also directly linked to emotional gratifications like happiness and love. Teaching your child social skills will enable him to develop friendships, maintain relationships, and help him become functional members of society.

Unfortunately, learning social skills and cues is a little harder for people with autism. They don't easily pick up the rules and customs that generally guide our interactions with people. And so, they sometimes need explicit instruction and a lot of attention to fully integrate. People with ASD often try to compensate by trying to figure out how society works by themselves. More often than not, their attempts at social interaction come off as unnatural, and they might even hurt and offend people. As their mentors, guardians, and parents, it's your duty to care for them by teaching them the appropriate social skills and rules they need to integrate with society, on their own terms.

Teaching social skills

Children with ASD differ immensely from one another, and it is impossible to take a single method or approach when you are attempting to teach them something as vital as social skills. Before you go on ahead to teach them what you assume is appropriate social skills, it's important to identify just what areas your child struggles with.

Here are four problmes that Children with ASD typically experience. They find it difficult to share how they feel or what they think with people, and they are sometimes oblivious to certain rules. They also sometimes have trouble using non-verbal communicative cues, as well as starting and maintaining relationships.

These four are the most popular problems, and we will explore how to approach them in the following pages. It is possible to experience other problems, but they are usually an extension of these base problems. For instance, if your child has trouble sharing toys or he is awfully directive and bossy, he probably has a problem sharing his feelings with people. After you have identified the social deficiency or deficiencies your child is experiencing, the next step is to address them with tried and tested methods of education. These typically include role-playing, practice play dates, visual cues, and video examples.

When teaching your child social skills, it's important to remember that you have to not only teach them the skills, you also have to tell them why you are teaching them. Children are a lot smarter than most parents think. Unless you really break it down to them and tell them why it might be offensive to not share something with someone, they can act out and be a bit difficult to handle.

You must always remember to be patient and be very gentle and meticulous. Positive reinforcement can considerably simplify the teaching process. Besides the fact that it boosts confidence, it can also be a great way to tell your child that he's making progress.

The Idea of developing social skills at home

Teaching your young one social skills is an exercise that you have to limit to your home. Family members like grandparents, godparents, and even siblings can help with their social education. It's important to act out real-life situations and teach them to react as appropriately as possible. Simply telling them won't be as helpful as showing them visually.

Visual learning by examples and visual stimuli will always produce better results. Therapists can also help with role-playing and playdates. Outsiders and experts are sometimes welcome, but it is recommended that you keep their physical involvement to a minimum. Children with ASD can often be scared, intimidated, or even hostile towards strangers. Keep the circle small.

Roleplaying

As we have already discussed, the visual stimulus is key, and nothing is quite as stimulating as recreating possible scenarios and teaching your child to utilize the appropriate social skills. Role-playing sessions can range from recreating comfortable situations and helping them tackle it better to introducing a potentially unfamiliar or scary situation and walking them through it.

For example, you could role play that you are a familiar person like his best friend from school, or you could play the dentist your child hates visiting. In both these scenarios, you could take breaks and tell him what to do and what not to do. It's important to introduce a little bit of adversary from time to time to challenge him. During role-playing sessions, you have to remember that it gets worse before it gets better. With enough practice, your young one will eventually understand and learn to deal with difficult situations.

Video examples

Video examples are perfect ways to explain social rules and cues like turn-taking, non-verbal communication, and sharing. You could pause the video to explain at certain intervals what exactly is happening between the speakers in the conversation and tell them what would be considered appropriate and not.

It could also be a very effective way to teach them how to start conversations, make friends, and maintain relationships. Video examples should also be occasionally paired with role-playing. You can use video examples to introduce the concepts and then reinforce them with role-playing and acting exercises.

Visual cues

Visual cues are a common and effective way to teach your toddler non-verbal communication and actionable social skills. It can help him identify and initiate complex reactions in appropriate situations. It can also teach him about conversational starters. For example, when they see someone stretching out their hands after introducing themselves, it could be an invitation to greet them by shaking their hands. Also, a hand stretched out with possibly a drink, food, or snack of some sort could be an invitation to eat. A frown could be a non-verbal indication that people want an apology of some sort or possibly a show of empathy. Open arms could be an invitation for a hug and a hand held out in front of a face could be a warning of some sort.

Practice play dates

Practice playdates are the final stage of teaching social skills. It allows your child to implement all the lessons, valuable skills, and tips he has been able to master during the course of your training. You could, for example, have introduced your young one to the concept of boundary intrusion and invite over his best friend to practice a life lesson with him. It throws a little bit of diversity into your usual lessons and it ensures that he is growing as a person.

Entering games and situations

Teaching non-verbal communication in conversations and maintaining it is one thing, but starting it is another thing entirely. It's important to teach your young ones all about entering conversations as naturally as possible so that they can achieve what they want from each interaction. To properly teach your child or kids what they need to start and maintain conversations, you need to teach him about conversational cues and conversational starters.

Conversation starters are ideas, imageries, and observations that typically indicate a shared interest or a great trait or feature. Conversation starters are really tricky, and it can be challenging figuring them out. But, with enough practice, they can be mastered and improved upon. The best types of conversation starters or topics are the ones both speakers know a little bit about. So, it could be anything from food to television programs, and even Santa Claus. Conversation starters can be considered rude if they point out a toxic or inappropriate habit a person does not want you pointing out. For example, a person with alcohol addiction might not want you asking it out. Most times, the appropriate conversational starter is usually a person's positive attribute or interest.

Conversational cues are verbal and non-verbal indications of a speaker's interest to either continue, change, or end a given topic of conversation. Like conversation starters, they can be sometimes difficult to get used to or master. Verbal expressions are the most common use of conversational cues. When a speaker indicates through speech that he needs to leave, or they ask you to talk about something else, they are expressing their desires going forward. You should teach your young ones the conversational meaning of these words through any of the chosen mediums we have discussed earlier.

Spotting non-verbal cues is a more complex task, especially as it relates to conversational cues. They usually entail some movements or facial signals. For example, when someone scratches their head or looks confused, it could be a great moment to consider changing the topic. Someone physically moving backward could be an indication of discomfort, or them trying to tell you they want to leave. You could teach your kids about nonverbal conversational cues by using video examples or even pictures.

You should also teach them about observing pleasantries when initiating conversations. Teach them how important it is to exchange pleasantries while introducing themselves to strangers that they like. Talk about how to effortlessly switch between conversations by identifying non-verbal and verbal conversational cues and choose a topic that they think the second speaker will like.

Coping with loss

Accepting loss of every kind is a vital part of growing up. Kids might not really understand loss on a grand scale, but an initiation to the concept is always better for children, especially children with ASD. If they are taught to accept a loss on a smaller scale earlier on, it becomes infinitely easier to handle it on a larger and more devastating scale.

Loss can come in any form. It doesn't have to be something as significant as losing the science fair or losing some competition; it could be losing at something as trivial as a game of tag. It is important to make them understand that everyone, even presidents, sometimes lose.

Winners lose too, and some of the biggest winners in history started as losers. The lesson would be the perfect time to tell them all about Abraham Lincoln. He was one of the best presidents that America ever had, and he started out losing every single political race he ever ran in. After using the president as a great role model of loss, teach them about dealing with loss. People will tease them and try to make them feel bad about themselves. It's important to teach them the importance of learning to be confident regardless of how mean kids are.

You can teach them mantras to recite whenever they are about to get upset. The mantras should contain words or things that they have faith in or really like. They should contain things that could help them focus on the positive, feel safe, remain grounded, and help them ignore bullies. Teach them the importance of never doubting themselves, as it is also an important part of learning to cope with loss. Try to remind them that minor losses like losing at tag don't matter as much as people think. The game is all about having fun. Teach them to focus on having fun and not winning. The less they care about winning or losing, the less upset they will be when they lose or win.

Social skills are difficult to master, period. It doesn't really matter if your child is on the autism spectrum or not. Childhood is a very sensitive period in a child's life. It forms the building blocks of a child's personality and even goes on to determine things like their personality, likes, dislikes, and fears. Teaching them helpful social skills will go a long way to reduce the pressure during this sensitive part of their development.

Chapter Three

COMMUNICATION

Communication is a basic human function that involves two or more people exchanging information through the use of language and other media. Communication doesn't necessarily have to entail words. Often times, words, phrases, and even sentences have covert meaning that only people who have had prior access to specific experiences are able to decode. Communication is expansive and to really understand it, you have to take a deep look at concepts like semiotics, semantics, and even pragmatics.

To children with ASD, communication can be quite confusing. Not all children will be able to speak eloquently or pick up on non-verbal communicative signals as well as other children. As a parent, it is important to come to terms with this. Understand your child's position on the spectrum and temper your expectations accordingly.

How they communicate and get your attention

People, in general, communicate verbally and non-verbally. In most cases, the verbal entails communicating through speech using a popular language that is shared both by the speaker and listeners. Furthermore, verbal communication is not only limited to languages. It can also be oral sounds. Babies, for example, don't communicate with any identifiable language; they just produce sounds and expect that their desires are understood by their caretakers or parents.

Non-verbal communication involves communicating without speech or sounds. It is the transmission of information through eye contact, gestures, posture, visual cues, and body language. Non-verbal communication is quite wide and perverse. There is an innumerable number of ways that we humans communicate. Most of these don't even involve sounds or language at all. Children with ASD primarily utilize verbal communication and very limited non-verbal communication when they pass information. They have a hard time picking up on covert communicative signals which is often what happens when a communicator chooses to switch to non-verbal communication. In some rare cases, children with ASD have incredible prowess when it comes to the non-verbal medium of communication, like sign language.

Every child has a unique communicative style. It is a vital part of their identity, and you must learn to identify this unique pattern and learn to predict what it really means. For example, if your child repeats certain words over and over again, it's no doubt for a good reason. This phenomenon is called Echolalia, and it is very common among children with ASD. It can happen for a lot of reasons, and in most cases, it is a way of telling you how they feel or what they want. If your child keeps repeating a phrase he heard on television, and it is tied to something tangible like an object, the odds are that he is trying to tell you that he wants that object.

Children with ASD also sometimes use made-up words and switch-up pronouns. It is a very normal way of navigating and ultimately mastering the language itself. As mentioned earlier, it's important to learn to read in-between the lines and anticipate their needs. Echolalia is the most popular verbal anomaly among kids with ASD, but it's not the only way children communicate their needs, emotions, or thoughts. You already know that children can also communicate their thoughts non-verbally. They can present them in the form of aggression, tantrums, or even repetitive habits. As with verbal communication, it's important to not get hung up over how bad your child's action is or the effect it might have on your self-image. Instead, focus on why your child did what he did and what is he trying to tell you. For example, when your child throws away a toy he does not like, it could be because it is disturbing him or making him feel uncomfortable. Try talking to him and get to the bottom of it. Knowing what goes on in your child's mind could potentially make all the difference down the line. Assistive devices also count as a form of communication. A child with limited control of a language can take a short cut with an assistive device and tell you precisely what he needs. There are great pictures in these apps that signify requests or actions, and when your child clicks on them, the parent/guardian can automatically know what the child needs.

Support communication development

It's common knowledge that children with autism have problems with the development of their communicative skills. They need support and constant help so that they don't end up deficient in certain areas. Communication is seen as a survival skill in most societies, and having limited control over your communicative abilities can be often regarded as a major disadvantage. As a parent, it's your duty to ensure that your child develops his communicative skills to the limit of his natural abilities. Let's look at some of the ways that you can stimulate great communicative growth.

One of them is to communicate by example. Children learn primarily by imitation. They are sure to copy you when they see you communicate or act in a certain way. When you communicate, make sure you always say what you mean and use the appropriate gestures. After seeing it a few times, they will learn to link the words, gestures, or movements with a particular object or concept. Children who use non-verbal communication as their primary mode of communication have to be taught sign language with special attention to gestures too. It's important not to skip any part of the communicative process. Since sign language is mostly hand gestures, you must always correct their mistakes and use the right signs all the time.

Integrate communicative media and teach them new skills from time to time. Even though a young child's mind is essentially an information sponge, it still needs some guidance. Like you would limit your child to the use of certain words and introduce others later on, you should also introduce communicative skills in the same manner. You should incorporate learning apps and tablets in this endeavor. There are thousands of great learning apps that simplify the learning process and break it down for your kids. You want them to completely master a previous skill before introducing a foreign or more complex skill.

Let your child have a little bit of real-world practice every once in a while. The only reason you teach your child complex language or communicative skills is so that he can use them in the appropriate situation in the real world. The real world is a lot less scary if you show him that it is. Gently wean him and let him talk whenever you visit the doctor or the restaurant.

Also, change the context whenever you can. The world is big and diverse, and in most cases, the textbook examples you have practiced with your child a thousand times won't be exactly what he comes across when he is communicating. As a communicative coach, you must understand that language is very context-specific, and different contexts require different approaches. It's not possible to exhaust all the possible contexts that a certain phrase might occur, but you can do a lot to limit your child's confusion. You can shake things up every now and again and introduce different locations, people, and times when you role-play.

A big part of bringing up your child is learning and growing as your child also learns and grows. As a parent, you should not be confused whenever your child does something or falls behind in some way. You need to be at your best if you want to keep up with your child's learning and growth.

How to encourage them to communicate

Motivating them to use language and other modes of communication is not only an excellent way to improve their language skills, but it is also a great way to help them overcome anxiety. The only way language skills can be developed is to use them as frequently as possible. Kids with ASD tend to keep to themselves. They are afraid that people won't understand them, so they choose not to speak at all. As their friend and guardian, you should try to get them to come out of their shell by initiating conversations about topics that they have shown interest in. You could use positive reinforcement to help them develop confidence in their communicative or language skills. It's a must that you try to get them to communicate as frequently as you are able. Ask about their day, what they like, who they have been talking to. All these things will help them get the practice they need to be able to achieve their interactional goals later on.

Imitating their speech patterns and behaviors is a type of positive reinforcement rooted in behavioral psychology. If you show them how fashionable their various sounds or characteristics are, they are less likely to doubt themselves later on. It also promotes continuous engagement, and it could possibly function as a correctional marker that indicates when they have strayed away from acceptable behavior. For example, imagine that you're playing an imitation game where you and your child repeatedly mimic one another. The moment you stop, they will notice and be able to surmise that is no doubt as a result of unacceptable behavior. Prompting your child to speak by directing questions to them and giving them non-verbal cues is an especially effective way to encourage them to talk or communicate more. When you ask them those questions, you are giving them opportunities to express themselves and put the knowledge they have acquired to good use.

Keeping the language simple and interesting is a quick and effective way to keep them talking. Explaining concepts and expressing yourself in words they can understand will encourage them to keep the conversation going because they feel like they are talking to someone they understand. Complex terminologies and big words can be scary regardless of what age your child is, so make sure you always carry them along when you talk. You can also keep them excited and talking if you discuss something they are interested in. Every child has a toy, animation, or cartoon they simply can't stop talking about. Once you figure out your kid's favorite thing, talk about it exhaustively.

Additionally, you should let therapists do some of the hard work for you. It can be tempting to try to do all the work yourself. But, therapists are professionals who have been specially trained to help your kids with their communicative troubles. It helps to let them do their jobs and take out some time for yourself. Children, in general, sometimes build up walls around themselves. They can be cautious of strangers and they isolate themselves from people if they don't feel comfortable. As a care provider, it's vital that you don't let your child become a recluse or introverted at such a young age. Their communication skills might suffer and they will have a hard time fitting into society. It's important to try to break down that shell with role-playing games, imitation, love, and delightful conversation whenever you can.

Chapter Four

BUILDING FUN ROUTINES

Raising an autistic child can be very challenging and sometimes, even overwhelming. It's important to make the best of the experience and see it as more of an adventure than a chore. Children are gifts, and incorporating fun and interesting routines can make the experience of raising them infinitely more fun for everyone involved.

Routines are a sequence of coordinated actions that are frequently repeated after predetermined intervals. Routines are supposed to be definite, structured, and mildly flexible. They are heavily coordinated and typically repeated after a period of time. Routines are used to manage complex and delicate events or objects. And since children are arguably some of the most complex and delicate beings on earth, you need a solid routine if you're going to be successful. One step out of place, and you can permanently derail your day, wasting time you don't have.

Creating a Fun Routine You Can Maintain

Routines are supposed to be built for sustainability and long-term use. This means creating a routine you can easily follow without too many exceptions. There are a number of things you should note when you are planning to draw out your first routine.

You should try to be very conservative with your time allocations and daily goals. Trying to accomplish too many things will cause spillovers, and that will cause your routine to fall apart. But, attempting to get it right the first time construct the routine is also quite presumptuous. Like most people, you'll find that the perfect routine is only found by trial and error. Don't get frustrated when it doesn't work out immediately. Instead, take time to learn from your mistakes with each failure.

Your schedule should start in the morning and end when your child goes to sleep. Children tend to be very active in the mornings. Therefore, you should make sure that you consider that in your routine. Set a little bit of extra time for morning tasks so that you have a cushion for those inevitable but unexpected outbursts. Tasks like preparing for school and having breakfast need some extra time. Ten minutes should be enough. But, don't be afraid to add more if your child requires it.

Also, create room for the occasional lesson when you are drafting your schedule. Kids get better at things with practice, so it's best to draft time for simple and complex communicative lessons throughout the day. You'll never know when you need to give a lengthy lesson about certain concepts. These lessons often require you to teach them immediately while the occurrence is still fresh in your child's mind. If you take too much time, you may miss the opportunity. Even though you can't anticipate periods like this, you can surely prepare for them when they crop up. And they always do.

Use a vision board to test run your potential routine ideas

A great way of cutting the learning curve in half and getting around to creating your first functional routine is to play out alternating scenarios in your head. You need to hypothesize frequently and run a lot of virtual scenarios in your head. You already know what you need to get done during the day. You also know what your child is like and how he reacts to certain things. You can create a schedule and imagine how it plays out. If you do it properly, you can immediately identify how the whole scenario can go wrong. Then, add some time cushion to see how it might make things better. You can also move things around by placing one event after the other.

Managing unexpected changes in routines

It is possible to draw or map out a nearly perfect routine that works most of the time. But you can't come up with something that will work all the time. Change is inevitable, and adults often welcome it with open arms. It can be scary for kids with autism. The unknown is heavily linked to danger and you should always try your best to normalize change by preparing them and yourself for the event or change to come. Put yourself in your child's shoes and imagine how he might react to the event and use the answers you get to plan towards the actual event.

There are two popular ways of dealing with a potentially triggering new experience. One is the one we just described, in which you can learn how to predict new and scary experiences and do damage control. This method requires you to teach your child to expect triggering things and show him how ordinary they are. The best way to normalize these things is to introduce them in a fun and non-threatening way. You can do this by using a storyboard or visual aid. You could swap items out with a picture of them and prepare a presentation detailing the features and the advantages of these ideas or conccpts.

The second method is dealing with the aftermath of those encounters by explaining what they are on the spot and teaching your child not to be afraid of it. You should come up with specialized routines that will help them manage a sudden change they can't quite understand. Creating a calming routine that they can walk through whenever they feel overwhelmed could potentially help you prevent outbursts and tantrums before they even happen. For example, a sudden visit to the emergency room can be very scary and confusing. It is only natural for your child to react by crying and throwing a tantrum. You could calm him down by asking him to initiate a calming routine you must have practiced time and time again. Going over several emotion control exercises prior to any confusing or trying change is an effective way to help your child accustom himself to the new realities he has just been exposed to.

As a parent, you ready know that children don't act out without a good reason, even if that reason doesn't make sense to you. Public explosions and tantrums are a sign of something deeper and uncomfortable. To adequately resolve sudden tantrums, you need to exploit your child's relationship with their favorite things. These could function as emotional comfort toys. Things like headphones, sunglasses, and toys could go a long way to alleviate the discomfort they feel and potentially defuse the situation before it gets out of hand. Calming exercises are also a great way to help them better handle scary situations. Activities like nature walks and yoga are a great way to help them practice being calm and in control. Moreover, breathing exercises are also an effective way to manage their outbursts or reactions.

Sometimes when children act out or they are afraid, all they really want is to feel comfortable and loved. You'd be surprised how powerful a parent's presence and love can be in sensitive moments. Empathy is key when you are trying to defuse very loud and public outbursts. Threatening them with punishment will only escalate the situation.

You need to show empathy and give them exactly what you would want if you were in their situation.

Though both methods are impressive in their own right, in isolation, they are not the best approach to deal with potentially scary and triggering situations. What is recommended is a combination of both methods. This way, if the lesson doesn't quite resonate with them, you could always calm them down afterward.

Planning for expected changes in routines

Change can come in all shapes and sizes, and it doesn't have to constitute something dramatic and life-changing. It could be something as trivial as a new cereal brand. Or it could be something as life-changing as going to a new school. Nine out of ten times, a child with ASD will find new changes and even slight alterations to a routine very scary, so that is why it is essential to plan ahead and better manage his reactions.

You could alleviate his fears by normalizing the entire experience through storytelling. A story about your experience with that new event could calm your child down. For example, if you plan to visit a new doctor with your child, tell him a story about your experience with a doctor and how it helped you, even though it was a bit frightening at first.

Create a visual timetable that warns them of any unexpected changes. Even though it is unexpected, seeing it move close and closer every day can sensitize your child to the change and make it easier to bear. You should consider investing in a beautiful graphic calendar so that they can physically see the events of the weeks to come ahead of time and consciously prepare themselves for the encounter. You can also create your own calendar. If you're unable to find one in a theme that your child loves, creating your own gives you the ability to do whatever you like with it. It may seem like a long and stressful process, but it may be worth it. It's as simple as talking to a graphics designer about what you really want to do.

Introducing something new can be a lot less trying and destabilizing for your child when you give him a lot of time to react and get accustomed to the news or change. You could show him pictures of what will happen at the new school, institution, or appointment. It is very important that your child is allowed to slightly normalize the events that are about to transpire. The more time your child has to react, the better. Changes are not always scary; they can be exciting too. Your child might absolutely fall in love with a new activity or game that they have been just recently introduced to. This is a lot more common than you think, and it can be managed effectively by introducing a timer and teaching your child to obey the timer. Each time you hear the timer go off, it could be a sign that it's time to stop whatever he is doing.

Changing your schedule slowly instead of suddenly can teach your child to accept change in a controlled manner. Perhaps you plan to teach your child to be a little bit more independent by showing him how to brush his teeth. You could slowly make him ready by letting him finish brushing.

Change in a schedule is not always either scary or exciting; it could also appear disinteresting. However, you can get your children to better accept this new seemingly boring change by linking it with something they find interesting. You could also generate interest by using praise and rewards to motivate more involvement. Changing your routine takes a lot of time, effort, and careful planning. You should always take great care when you plan out a single routine alteration, and you should try to predict your young one's reaction and plan for it dutifully. Changing your schedule doesn't have to be an overly complicated thing. It can be simple, straightforward, and delightfully uneventful.

Reward flexibility

Routine gives structure and helps kids with autism maintain control over different areas of their lives. It can be very influential and could keep them grounded and calm most of the time. It could also, however, be a limitation. It is important that they learn and understand the place of flexibility and see the advantages that come with it. As a parent, if your child learns to be flexible, that will ensure that you experience fewer public episodes and you save more time. It could also be great for the child too. Flexibility allows them to handle new and scary situations with less fear and more control. This could grossly benefit their social skills and reduce the innate fear of the unknown.

In general, the benefits of flexibility are immense. For you, as a parent, it gives you more comfort and confidence in your child's ability to behave himself in public places. Ironically, flexibility can help you establish more order and control over the activities. For your child, achieving flexibility is a very important milestone to reach. And once he does, he can progress to higher and more complex ones. It basically enhances his development.

You should realize that getting your child to embrace flexibility doesn't necessarily mean that you expose him to new and scary situations. You can start off by complementing and rewarding him each time he encounters something new or does something different. You could reward him by giving him more playtime, increasing his gadget time, or giving him healthy snacks.

Things not to do when your child is throwing a tantrum because he is afraid

An episode is bound to happen sooner rather than later for most kids with autism. As a parent, you've probably already encountered something like that. It varies depending on your child's mood, but it will involve a variety of cries, yells, and maybe even throwing of toys. When it is caused by fear or discomfort, there are a number of things you should try to avoid it.

The first thing you should try to avoid is raising your voice at him. When a child throws a fit in public because he is scared, the last thing you want to do is yell. All you'll end up doing is stoking the flames and making it that much harder to deal with him later on. The second thing you should never do is get nervous. Getting nervous during a meltdown will cloud your mind and let you choose the worst possible solution to the problem your child is experiencing.

Thirdly, don't get embarrassed. Admittedly, it can be very embarrassing to deal with your child's tantrum in public. But, you have to remember that your child is the one in pain and not the bystanders. They are merely spectators, and they don't matter as far as you are concerned. Focus on your child and let everyone whine and complain as much as they want.

Finally, don't forget to reward him when he calms down eventually. Children respond to reward more than they respond to punishment. Always show them that you appreciate their effort by rewarding their efforts accordingly. Establishing a routine that works for your child is a vital part of parenting. You might need some time and testing, but you will figure it out eventually. And when you do, your job will be much easier.

Chapter Five

PARENTS' GUIDE

Up until this chapter, this book has focused heavily on children with autism. We have talked about helping them overcome some of their biggest fears and limitations, but we haven't really focused on the parents, guardians, and anybody that has to live with raising a child with autism. The CDC estimates that one in 88 families has a son or daughter with autism. This means all over America, families everywhere have to deal with that new reality without prior warning or preparation.

This new information can be very trying and scary. So much so that it's enough to rip families apart and force kids to grow up in broken homes. It's not uncommon to see parents drift apart, because of the stress of parenting children in general. If you add caring for a child with autism to the mix, what you have is a situation that most people would rather run away from. As parents, you are expected to be able to tackle whatever might come your way without hesitation or ever slowing down, but humans are not just built like that. You need to take time to process all the new things that you are just learning, and prepare yourself for the arduous journey ahead, instead of pretending that everything is fine. In this chapter, we will be focusing on parents and guardians for a change. We'll talk about how you can deal with the diagnosis and parenting a child with autism.

Response to the diagnosis

Parents who know very little about the autism spectrum are sure to be the most sensitive to the news. It's usual that parents get afraid and angry when they learn that their child was born with a condition that has been stigmatized for a long time now. But, it is not as limiting or as challenging you might fist think. However difficult this is to acknowledge and recognize, you must recognize this and try not to have a full-blown meltdown in the doctor's office upon finding out that your life is about to change forever. Some things will change but some things will also remain the same. Your baby is still your baby, and a disorder shouldn't cause you to see him in a different light.

Autism can make communication difficult for a child, but it doesn't have to be that way. New colleges, researches, and institutes dedicated to helping kids with autism have been springing up in recent times all over the world. More progress has been made in the past twenty years than there has been in the past century. There hasn't been a better period in history for your child to come into the world than right now because the resources are readily available for you to raise him in the most normal way possible. So relax because it's not going to be as bad as you think. With the right help and environment, your child will lead a long, healthy and productive life.

Once you've realized that all the help you could ever need is waiting for you, the next step is to find out the specific kind of help you need in your situation. There are literally millions of great doctors, schools, and specialists waiting for you. The only way to adequately exploit these exciting new opportunities is to make sure you are adequately informed. Do a lot of research and read about terminologies, laws, and special rights. You should investigate terms like individualized education programs, least restrictive environment, early intervention, Individuals with Disabilities Education Act, Free Appropriate Public Education, etc.

Know what is good and what's outdated. Read journals and immerse yourself in the literature available. Search for websites online and join support groups you think can actually help you.

Neurologists and therapists say that the first three years are the most crucial for a child with autism. Their mind is still highly malleable, and a lot of progress can be made within that period. During those crucial years, it is important that you get him all the help that you can find. Get a team of doctors and book an appointment with specialists and therapists who are at the top of their profession. You'll also need the help of other relevant professionals like pediatricians, neurologists, biomedical experts, psychical therapists, and speech therapists. Regularly consult with each of these professionals whenever you feel you might need them and keep the relationship fresh and thriving.

Raising an autistic child can be a fun and transformative experience. It forces you to go out of your comfort zone and improve as a person. Raising an autistic child sometimes means becoming an amateur therapist yourself. Simple yet effective therapy methods like the Applied Behavior Analysis, The Floortime Method, the rapid prompting method, the Picture Exchange Communication System, the Verbal behavior analysis, and the sensory diet method are a few of the new and exciting skills you might have to learn to help your child with his communicative and social integration challenges. The therapy styles mentioned here are just a few of the popular styles of instruction. Utilizing a single method is not advised. There is a plethora of methods out there, and you should always utilize all the information and resources at your disposal. They could sometimes be the key to overcoming the latest plateau in your child's communicative journey.

Getting the best doctors, specialists, and therapists is not going to be cheap. One of the most important steps in the reaction and preparation process is figuring out a financial plan that works for you. It is estimated that caring for a person with autism through their lifetime could cost about $3 million dollars; it is more than what some families make in a decade. Handling this new financial burden can bear heavily on a family, especially if only one of the parents is working. It is recommended that families who are not financially equipped to handle the expense out of pocket should turn to the government and great insurance policies to help lessen the burden. There are extensive relief laws and benefits accessible to families in over 25 states in America. Parents and caretakers should also look into cutting down costs by getting rid of expenses they can learn to do without. The crucial point here is that financial planning is a necessary and difficult part of planning for your new lives as parents. It can be extremely demoralizing, and it is always better to jump on it as soon as you can.

While parenting a child with autism, you should learn to keep a journal of your child's progress. Raising a child with autism can be tough and tiring. Sometimes, all the challenges can make you focus on only the negative part of your child's journey. That is why keeping a journal of progress and treatment plans is important. Not only does it serve as a reminder of how far you and your child have come, but it also provides information that you might need at a later time. From where you are now, it can be very difficult going through all the motions and transitioning from panicking to keeping a journal. As you go transform from shocked to proactive parents, it's important to remember where you started from. The proper initial reaction is important, and you must remember that your decision and state of mind must never prevent your child from getting the help he needs.

Your role as a parent

The society might think you are unlucky, and you might feel down the first few months of learning about your child's condition, but you have a responsibility as a parent. Admittedly, it is a lot more demanding to raise a child with autism. But, you are a parent nonetheless, and there are certain responsibilities that you must attend to.

The first is the role of the caretaker. As a parent, you are a caretaker by default. You are automatically responsible for the bundle of joy you call your child. Unfortunately, the responsibility of the caretaker is, however, magnified with an autistic child. The cost of care significantly goes up, and you should be ready for the never-ending medical bills that he will incur in his lifetime. You need to be prepared for this added cost. It will be your duty to cater to all nutritional and medical needs that he might have.

You may not realize this, but you're also your child's new best friend. No one is going to spend more time with him than you are. As his best friend, you must learn to cater to his emotional needs and really concentrate on understanding and helping him. As his best friend, it is also your duty to introduce him to new and scary concepts too. The world can be a big and scary place, and handling introductions can make it more tolerable for your child.

You are also the resident authority figure. A lot of parents assume that their autistic needs and wants are absolute. They sometimes spoil them and refuse to say no every once in a while. Autistic kids are still kids. They may not communicate in ways that you are used to, but they communicate all the same. As parents, you shouldn't spoil your kid by giving him everything he wants. The result will be the same as when you give a child everything he asks for, even though he doesn't really need it. The child will become entitled and disrespectful. Since your duty involves raising your child right, saying no is actually a great way to do that. Learn to say no every once in a while. It will make them less dependent and teach them a little bit about how the real world works.

Coping with the situation

Did you know that many parents find it difficult to accept that their kids are really autistic? It's simply easier to accept that it's a phase that he can grow out of. But, autism is a permanent condition, and your child will have to live with it for the rest of his life. And you, as a parent, also have to deal with that. It often takes several years for most people to really accept their new reality; some people end up never really understanding or accepting it.

Most parents either blame it on their genes or on bad parenting. They think it's somehow their fault because they didn't pay enough attention in the first few months of the child's life, or because they have a history of autism in their family, or something else along that line. They feel it's important to blame someone or something tangible. They often also feel a profound sense of loss and sometimes even mourn their child as if he died and was reborn as someone else.

Other parents outright deny that their child is autistic. They choose to get a second opinion and consult as many doctors and specialists as they can find. These kinds of parents want someone to lie to them and tell them everything is going to be okay.

Regardless of what category you as a parent might fall into when you find out about your child, it's important to go through a grieving process.

Grieving doesn't necessarily mean you are mourning your child; it's more about accepting that your child is no longer the person you thought he was. It's about consciously trying to accept the new realities that you are facing as a new parent. It's about letting go of whatever you thought was your truth and becoming the person your child needs you to be. The grieving process typically involves a period of fear, distress, denial, and even anger – all of these emotions are natural as part of the process. What is most important is that you experience all those scary emotions and let them end with the grieving process.

While you grieve, try to remember that autism is completely natural. There is nothing wrong with your child. You aren't cursed or unlucky or something like that. You shouldn't also let it cause you to neglect your other children because you are always so focused on one. Your other children deserve as much love as your autistic child. We will discuss more about balancing out your parental care among your children in chapter 9.

Grieving is different for everybody. Some people just slap it on and slap it off, and others end up grieving for much longer. Most people fall into the second category. It is okay to take the time to properly understand your new reality. What is important is that you are making an effort to accept your new reality.

How to avoid stress and taking care of yourself

Take a personal day every once in a while. People often say that parents don't get days off, but maybe they should. Taking care of and worrying about your children can get very tiring after a few months without rest. Why not take a personal day every once in a while to really cool off and get back your groove. Having a child with autism doesn't mean he is your entire world. A little bit of distance can benefit both of you.

You are in a committed relationship; you could let your partner take the steering wheel for a day or two. It doesn't even have to be a long break, but it should just be long enough to help you unwind. Taking a trip with the family is also an excellent way to take care of yourself and the family at the same time. A retreat to a cabin or a summer home could be a wonderful way to get your child away from the city noises and fumes. During this retreat, you could work on things like their communication and social skills. Decompressing with periodic trips to the spa is a wonderful way to remain stress-free. Spending a day with your friends doing what you enjoy is another therapeutic exercise that you should try often. It might not be as pleasurable as taking a short sabbatical, but it could work just as well.

You could also get a hobby. Hobbies are affordable stress-relieving activities that can help you cool off after a long and arduous day. The hobby you choose could be anything. You can also have a passion every once in a while. Most parents have their go-to comfort item or accessory. For some, it is food, and for others, it's a drink. Whatever your comfort accessory is, learn to rely on it when you feel stressed or you feel like spoiling yourself. A little bit of self-care can go a long way.

Chapter Six

HELPING YOUR CHILD WITH AUTISM THRIVE

Helping your child thrive is a very important part of parenting a child with autism. Parents need to make special accommodations for their autistic children since their development pattern isn't going to follow the normal route. These accommodations will involve finding new ways to connect and communicate with your child. Granted, this can be quite difficult if you've raised other children without ASD. But, all it requires is knowledge of a new way of doing things. You can think of it as parenting 2.0. Besides learning how to communicate, you'll also need to provide an environment where your child can be free to play and express himself without risks of injury. This includes childproofing the house, as well as a few extra precautions.

After your visit with the doctor and subsequent diagnoses, you'll most likely receive some form of education on how to proceed. This will include helping you locate support and help, as well as creating a treatment plan. This chapter addresses all of these points in detail. Let's begin with one of the most important factors, i.e. providing structure and safety.

Provide structure and safety

First, we'll address the matter of structure. Even though you're almost as new to dealing with autism as your child is, you can't use that as an excuse. If you're going to provide structure, you'll need to learn as much as you can about the condition. We've already addressed this in previous chapters. With sufficient knowledge on the condition, you can learn to be consistent.

Consistency is one of the most important structures you can provide for your child. The reason is that children with ASD often have difficulty transferring lessons from one sphere to the other. So, if your child learns something in school, applying the same lessons at home won't come naturally. A very typical example is sign language. Children with ASD may learn the basics in school but never think to use it to communicate at home. Here, consistency is all about keeping your child in the cycle of learning. You should find out what he is learning in school or at the therapist's and find a way to continue the techniques at home.

Another useful trick is to let your child learn in more than one environment. If you have therapy sessions in the doctor's office, try scheduling one at home. The change of environment can encourage your child to transfer skills and knowledge from one scenario or environment to the other.

Another important part of providing structure for your child is creating and sticking to a schedule. Children with ASD thrive best in highly structured environments. The reliable and repetitive nature of their daily tasks can help keep them focused. Your schedule should cover meal times, therapy sessions, school, playtime, and bedtime. The key here falls back to consistency. You have to stick to the schedule if it's going to work. You should try to keep disruptions to a bare minimum. Avoid them totally, if you can. If you observe that disruption is inevitable, you should prepare your child for it in advance and try to make it work around the structure. We already discussed this at length in chapter 4. You can refer to it for more information or for a refresher.

The next point on the issue of creating structure is rewarding good behavior. Positive reinforcement is very important when raising children with ASD. So, one of your responsibilities will be to observe good deeds that your child does. Even if the action was unintentional, praises could encourage the child to repeat it. Besides praises, other rewards include letting the child play with his favorite toy and giving him stickers.

Now, let's discuss the subject of safety. Earlier on, we discussed how raising a child with autism is like practicing parenting 2.0. The same analogy applies here because providing a safe home environment is going to go beyond any child-proofing you might have done in the past. This, however, doesn't mean you won't need the basic child-proofing measures like storing dangerous drugs and solutions on high shelves, and covering electrical outlets.

Some other safety precautions include safeguarding your windows by replacing the glass with Plexiglas, a more resistant, shatter-proof alternative. You should also put locks and alarms on all the doors where appropriate. This is more important if your child likes to wander. Placing locks and alarms will prevent your child from wandering and notify you when your child does so. As a part of the parenting 2.0 precaution, you should inform your local police and fire department of your child's tendency to wander. Also, inform them of the ASD and all the accommodations that you and your child will need.

Find nonverbal ways to connect

The most challenging aspect of raising a child with ASD is connecting with the child. But, the good news is that you don't have to speak to connect with your child. Simple non-verbal cues like the way you look at your child, the way you touch your child, and even the tone of your voice, can do all the communicating for you. As a parent, your child is constantly communicating with you in his own unique way, even though you may not recognize it. Increasing the strength of your connection can be as simple as learning how your child communicates and getting on board.

Your child will most likely communicate with you in subtle ways, using body language and facial expressions. You should pay attention to the sounds your child makes when he wants something, is hungry, or even tired. You also need to figure out why he does the things he does. Like all children, your child is going to throw a tantrum, and you're going to have to handle it. Children with ASD are often misunderstood due to the way they communicate, and so, they may get angry or frustrated more easily.

This lack of understanding, more often than not, will lead to a tantrum. Also, similar to the way most children behave, children with ASD will throw a tantrum to get attention and pass a message across. Honing your ability to pick up on their non-verbal cues is a great way to avoid these tantrums altogether. If you remember in chapter one, we discussed why children do the things they do. Sometimes, it's a cry for help. Other times, your child is simply trying to communicate with you and you don't seem to be getting the message. The tantrum can be a way of showing frustration. Understanding this can improve communication between the two of you.

While talking about the schedule, we discussed creating time for fun. Children who live with ASD are still children, and so, they're going to love to play their little hearts out. You need to create an environment where your child can do that as comfortably and happily as possible. You can't fill his days with therapy sessions and lessons. That will only inhibit his natural expression. When creating a schedule, the time for play should be around the period when your child is most awake and alert. You want him to have the most fun in the space of time.

While playing with your child, figure out creative ways to make him smile and laugh. Don't try to sneak any therapy or lessons into your playtime, as your child is bound to have much more fun if it doesn't look like another lesson. This playtime will be very therapeutic for your child. It will also help you connect in new and often unexpected ways.

One of the most common symptoms experienced by children with ASD is increased sensitivity to sensory stimuli. You need to pay special attention to see if your child has any of these hypersensitivities. Light, smell, sound, taste, and touch all have the potential to cause discomfort. In some other cases, children with ASD have a decreased sensitivity to these stimuli and will need more input if they are going to recognize them. Try to figure out what stimulations affect your child's behavior. Take note of those that elicit a positive reaction and those that elicit a negative reaction. Which stimuli are stressful and which ones are enjoyable? If you understand these, you can communicate and connect with your child in a much better way. It'll also be easier to determine the source of any difficulties your child might have.

Create a personalized autism treatment plan

Another key point in helping your child thrive is seeking suitable treatment. This step is very crucial because treatment sessions are supposed to be a constant part of your child's life. Unfortunately, there are so many treatment options that finding the most appropriate one can be very difficult. More difficult is the fact that everyone's going to try to offer you some kind of advice regarding the best way to go about your treatment. You can expect to hear conflicting inputs from friends, teachers, and even doctors. It is important to keep in mind that there isn't a single treatment plan that's suitable for every child with ASD. The most effective is usually a combination of several activities, and it should be based on your child's peculiarities. The treatment should consider your child's interests, strengths, and weaknesses.

There are multiple factors that an effective autism treatment plan will consider. The treatment must build on your child's interests, and it must offer a schedule that is predictable and achievable. It must also begin by teaching your child a series of simple tasks, broken up into steps. Whatever plan you choose must also engage your child and provide regular positive reinforcements. Lastly, no treatment plan is adequate if it does not actively involve you in your child's management.

It's better to understand your child to some degree before deciding on a treatment plan. This is because you need to answer basic questions about your child and use the answers to tailor the treatment. Questions like, "What are your child's strengths?" "What behaviors are most bothersome to you and your child?" "What skills does your child lack the most?" "What's the most effective way for your child to learn?" and of course, "What does your child enjoy doing?" Any treatment plan that takes these questions into account will be suitable.

Besides asking questions that relate to you and your child, you should also ask questions that relate to the treatment. Speak to as many treatment experts as possible and do an exhaustive amount of research. The treatment plan should be goal-oriented, and this, in itself, already makes the decisions easier for you. You don't have to choose one particular type of treatment. As long as it addresses your child's needs, you can combine a couple of therapy options.

Some of the common treatments include behavioral therapy, play-based therapy, physical therapy, occupational therapy, speech and language therapy, and nutritional therapy. It's obvious that no single therapy on this list will address all of your child's needs. So, you must employ quite a few for the best results. As a final thought in this segment, you should never design a treatment plan that's not sustainable. Your child's schedule should not be packed with activities that they don't enjoy or can't do consistently. Also, to avoid overwhelming your child, consider breaking the treatments up. Focus on learning the skills that are essential first, and you can handle the rest later.

Find help and support

Parenting is, no doubt, one of the toughest jobs in the whole world. Being a parent to a child with ASD can be twice as stressful as regular parenting. The processes of observing your child, picking up cues, and adhering to a schedule can demand a lot of time and energy. It's very common to feel overwhelmed on a lot of days. Thus, it is very important for you to find the time to take care of yourself. You can only give your child the best care when you're in good physical and mental condition. You shouldn't try to do everything on your own. And you certainly don't have to. It's clear that taking care of a child with ASD is a lot, and seeking help is only natural. In fact, it is recommended.

There are several opportunities you can exploit as a parent when it comes to seeking help and support. You can visit ADS support groups, for example. ADS support groups are a great opportunity for you to socialize and meet other families that are in the same situation as you are. You can share information, advice, and observations with each other. These other families will also be available to you for support and encouragement when you need it. You will also get the opportunity to provide support for parents who recently received a diagnosis. Knowing what they are going through, you can be a source of strength for them.

The second source of support you can explore is respite care. There are facilities that provide respite care for parents with autistic children. In respite care, you can have another caregiver take care of your child for some of time, giving you the opportunity to rest and recover.

As a parent, you're also entitled to counseling and therapy. If you feel like the process of caring for your child is overwhelming you, you may want to see a therapist of your own. In therapy, you can be expressive and discuss how you feel, your insecurities, and your fears. You can also seek family therapy for problems you might have in your own relationship. After all, caring for the autistic child is as much your responsibility as it is the responsibility of everyone in your family.

If you live in the United States, your child can also receive help through the Early Intervention Program. The program is available for infants up until the age of two. Before you can qualify for care under the Early Intervention Program, your child must undergo a free evaluation. If the evaluation reveals a developmental problem, the program's treatment providers will help you develop an individualized service plan. For children over the age of three, aid is available through school-based programs. They can be placed in groups for children with delayed development.

Chapter Seven

PRACTICAL SOLUTIONS TO EVERYDAY PROBLEMS

So far, we've covered many of the subjects you need to understand as a parent with an autistic child. In this chapter, we're going to tackle practical problems that you can expect to face every day and likely solutions to them. These are problems that regular parenting tips can't really help you with. For example, eating and sleeping. Children with ASD can be quite picky about their food. They can be even pickier than non-autistic children. You need to be able to apply all the principles you've learned so far for dealing with the problem. It's needless to say that you can't yell at them or tell them they have to eat it because you say so.

The same thing goes with problems with sleeping. Creating a schedule isn't enough to get your child to go to sleep. The chances are that your child doesn't even understand the concept of a schedule. It becomes your responsibility to ensure that the schedule is followed to the letter. Let's go over some of the problems you can expect to face, as well as practical solutions you can apply to solve them.

Eating

Some children with ASD are very limited in their dietary choices. They may only want to select two or three options. And unfortunately, none of these options might be viable from a dietary standpoint. You'll remember that nutritional therapy is a part of the treatment plan for children with ASD. This limited dietary list of choices presents you with a dilemma.

The first thing to do is to nip the problem in the bud. If you observe that your child progressively rejects a food, you need to end the trend as quickly as possible. If not, your child will limit the list of choices of food to a very few, often unhealthy options. If you let this happen, it will become even more difficult for you to get your child to eat healthy foods. But, to begin this process, you should start by choosing foods closest to your child's preferences. For example, if your child will not take a meal without strawberry ice-cream, the best approach is to begin by feeding your child strawberries. For some other scenarios, the texture of the food may be more important than the taste. For example, if your child likes potato chips, add corn chips to the food to mimic the texture.

Understandably, you're going to be concerned about the nutrition of your child. In that case, you should give your child multivitamins. They can provide additional nutrition that your child lacks in the corn-chips laden diet.

Next, you're going to need to take baby steps when introducing your child to new foods. This is very important because children with autism are very resistant to new foods. A great first step is to simply place the new food on your child's plate. Even though it might potentially turn the dinner table into a battlefield, you should still take the first step. You can remove the food after a few seconds if you need to. If your child tolerates the first step, give a reward. Rewards can vary, depending on what your child loves, but the common ideas are warm praises and hugs. You can also give small amounts of preferred food, like strawberry ice-cream, or doing a preferred activity.

Moving forward, take more baby steps like having your child smell the food, touch the food, bring the food towards the lips, and so on. The point of these steps is to gradually sensitize your child towards the food. Introducing it all at once will almost always lead to disaster. But, you certainly can't feed your child ice-cream and pizza for the rest of his life. Simple steps like tasting the food every now and then, and maybe mixing it with other favorite foods, can help your child get accustomed to the meal.

Finally, you should understand that you're probably not going to succeed in the first attempt. In fact, if you're a normal parent, you might not succeed for the first few attempts. The key is all in taking baby steps. You want your child to get accustomed to the idea of the food, no matter how long it takes. Also, if you reward your child with every successful step, you can associate the food with good feelings, and that can further help your cause.

Sleeping

One of the most challenging things about parenting a child with autism is getting them to go to sleep and stay asleep. Even though other parts of parenting are tough, this exacts a special toll on you as a parent. If your child doesn't sleep, you can't sleep. And sleep deprivation will only lead you to a downward spiral of unproductivity and stress. If you're having trouble de-stressing and taking care of yourself, you should refer back to chapter 6, where we talk about finding help and support.

The good news is that many of the tips we've discussed in this book can help you. The most significant of these is establishing a schedule and sticking to it. A bedtime routine can do a lot for you and your child. On a psychological level, it can signal the body that it's time to suspend all activities and recharge. These signals can be very comforting for a child with ASD, someone who is trying to make sense of all the sensory stimulation they are getting from their environment.

For this to truly work, you need to establish a routine that you will adhere to every single time. The order isn't as important as the routine itself. You can begin by telling your child that it's time for bed and proceed to the bathroom for brushing. Then comes the pajamas, then comes the bedtime stories, and then lights out. You can have it in whatever order you want, but the most important thing is to stick to the order every single time. You can also create a graph or some sort of visual aid to assist your child in remembering the specific order of things. With the passage of time, as your child gets used to it, going to bed will become less stressful.

Another helpful tip is to reduce rough and rowdy play as bedtime approaches. As the night falls, your child should be winding down from the day's activities, not getting riled up. Even though there should still be room for play and fun, depending on your schedule, it shouldn't agitate your child. Plays like tickling, wrestling, and roughhousing will definitely delay bedtime. Calmer activities like coloring or reading a bedtime story should dominate the hours before bed.

After you finally get your child to bed, the next course of action is to ensure that they can sleep comfortably. This includes precautions like mummy bags and night lights. Children with autism, and all children, in general, love to be swaddled and cuddled. The mummy bag has the same effect on the children, which is a very relaxing experience for them. Nightlights can also provide comfort for children, especially for those who are afraid of the dark. A nightlight with a very dim glow can provide comfort. Bright light may keep your child awake, which is not something you want.

The following tip goes without saying, but it's always better to say. Comfortable bedding is an absolute necessity. As an adult, it's very difficult to get a good night's sleep on an old and worn-out bed. Similarly, it's even tougher for children with autism to sleep on such a bed. The same thing applies to bedsheets and pillows.

Toilet training

Toilet training is one of the domestic activities that can really show how challenging it is to raise a child with autism. Some children can easily learn to use the toilet by the age of 5. But, it could take children with ASD up to 9 years to be fully toilet trained. However, since it is a spectrum, some children will pick up toilet training quicker than others. Some tips can help you toilet train your child quicker than you would without them. Let's go over these tips and see how you can apply each of them in training your child.

An important step is to clear your time and schedule. Toilet training is a very involving process, especially for children with ASD, and you need to be ready to commit to the process. New illnesses, moving, a new baby and any other major changes to the family dynamic can disrupt the training process for you and your child. You also have to release yourself from any sources of stress or pressure. Pressure from friends, family members, and even therapists to train your child can make the process more difficult for you. You may not realize it now, but toilet training can be a very long, and even emotional process. You wouldn't want to deal with all these other things during toilet training.

The next tip works closely with the first, and it is that you need to look out for when your child is ready for potty training. Age will not influence this discernment because children with ASD have developmental delays that separate them from normal children. The signs you should look for are staying dry throughout the night and asking to be changed. When your child becomes conscious of the discomfort associated with toilet matters, it shows that they are ready to use the big boy's toilet.

Once you observe that your child is ready to be toilet trained, you should begin loading him with fluids. Find out how much fluids your child can safely take in a day from your pediatrician, and ensure that your child gets the maximum dosage every single day. You can mix the water with juice and milk. The more fluids your child drinks, the more likely he is to urinate. While loading your child with fluids, ensure that you have all the things you need. You can even consider bringing toys or a TV screen to the bathroom. The key is to make your child comfortable on the toilet seat. Other things you can do include wrapping the toilet seat with towels for extra cushion or getting a potty seat that has handles.

To potty train a child, you need to make sure that the child sits on the toilet until the magic happens. You can take short breaks every now and then, but the child should sit for as long as possible. Eventually, the child will urinate in the toilet. When that happens, you need to give as much praise as you possibly can. Do whatever you can to show how proud you are of your child's achievement.

Next, you need to focus your attention on bowel movements. If your child sits on the toilet long enough, you'll eventually get a good bowel movement. In some cases, your child might be more open to pooping in diapers than pooping in the toilet. In this case, you'll want to begin by calculating when your child is likely to poop. Have your child poop with the diaper on while in the bathroom as a first step. Next, have him poop with the diaper on the toilet seat. Then, progress to him pulling his pants down before sitting on the toilet. Finally, have him poop with the diaper off. These steps may take a while, depending on your child, so it's a good idea to break them into smaller steps.

Public places

The challenge of handling a child with autism is different in public places because you will often have to deal with judging stares and explaining your situation to other people. The whole situation is often escalated when your child decides to have a meltdown in a public place, like a restaurant, for example. Handling situations like that often require you to understand your child's position. Remember that you've already established a strict routine for him to follow. Taking him out of that routine and into a new environment can be very disturbing for your child. At some level, you have to expect your child to be uncomfortable with the change. It's only natural. Your focus should be less on what people might say or think, and more on how you can help your child accommodate the new environment.

You should not feel embarrassed by your child unless the comments and stares actually have a foundation. Unless your child is actually acting inappropriately, you should hold your head high. Remember that your child is going through intense discomfort, and people who don't understand what your child is going through cannot possibly make a comment or contribution.

Also, you should understand that like everything else, taking your child to public places takes practice or baby steps. Start in your house and mimic some of the things you can expect to meet in the restaurant. Invite your kids into the kitchen while you cook. This will give them a different perspective about food in general, and it's not unlike what you'll see in the restaurant. You can also invite some family over and try to make it as conservative and, for lack of a better term, noisy as possible. You can expect the restaurant you visit to be noisy, so having a noisy dinner at home is not out of place.

As the next baby step, go to places where there are a lot of people, but only spend a small amount of time there. You could go to a department store or a supermarket to pick up some groceries. Once your child tolerates these visits well, you can proceed to have a short sit down at a café or diner. Remember that the key is to make your child acquainted to the experience. The trick is that since there are fewer people in a diner, there is lesser sensory input for your child and a smaller chance that he'll act up.

After doing all your practice runs and you feel like you're ready for the real deal, you have to be prepared for things to go out of control. Remember that your child is still a child, and he may not always behave in a way that you expect. You need to be accommodating enough to tolerate whatever behavior you see, and be prepared to handle it. In essence, you need an escape route. You need to estimate ahead of time how quickly you can pay the bill and get your child to the car.

Chapter Eight

LEARNING & TRANSITIONS

One of the major questions new parents have is, what really goes on in the mind of a toddler? They may appear cute and oblivious to the onlooker, but in a few short years, they undergo major changes and basically master language. Even experienced parents have only been able to come up with behavioral theories. Most of them don't really understand how toddlers interact or learn from the world around them.

Toddlers go through a number of phases within the early years of childhood. They learn intuitively and become independent a lot faster than one would expect. For most toddlers, communication and, by extension, self-expression, is an uninterruptable part of maturation. But for kids with autism, it's an entirely different process. You have to pay more attention to their development and try to get ahead of any notable deficiencies.

Depending on when you got your diagnosis, the attention you pay to every part of the communicative and social maturation process of their growth will vary. Toddlers are curious beings who learn primarily through play, sharing, exploration, and stimuli. Everything they do is loaded with meaning, and unless you learn to identify and nurture every aspect of their growth and transition, it can be very easy to lose track of time and let such a delicate period of their life pass you by.

Play

When a toddler crawls around and plays with his favorite toy, it is part of an elaborate learning process that involves testing the physical laws that guide the world he now finds himself in. What might seem like a drool-filled exercise that involves repeatedly trying to fit items into his mouth is simply an attempt to understand the concept of food and satiation.

Toddlers are humans in their most curious form. Play allows for toddlers to find answers to most of the questions they have, and it allows for the development of crucial survival skills. As you know, children learn how to walk by crawling around all day and finally getting around to walking. Play allows kids to build up experience, muscle, and gather direct information by watching more adults do it firsthand. Toddlers don't do much every day except work on their coordination, muscle control, balance, and strength. What might look like play to most adults is actually a complex and necessary physical and mental development exercise.

Play teaches them about physics, gravity, pain, and a lot of other fundamental laws and truths. Play allows toddlers to come in contact with different objects in their environment and learn from it through adaptation. A child understands on some level how gravity works by tossing around toys and other objects. He learns that once something goes up, it always comes down. Play lets them figure out how the strange, new world around them ultimately works.

There is a general rule about practice and mastery. It has to do with the repetition of a particular action obsessively until you can be said to have total mastery of the skill you are practicing to use. If a child is trying to develop language skills, the only way he is ever going to learn to talk is by babbling and speaking half sentences.

Finally, play allows children to use their imagination. Developing an active imagination is an essential part of a child's physical and emotional development. Their imagination teaches them to see the world through a different lens, and it allows their creative side to flourish. Materials like bricks and Legos are perfect for an imaginative child. Playing make-belief allows them to explore concepts like substitution and creation, and it tunes their fine motor skills while helps their minds learn.

Sharing is an often complex part of development. Most children pick up on it eventually, while others require a push in the right direction. As a child develops, his mind undergoes numerous changes, and at a point, he will be able to fathom complex emotional cues just from watching parents and caretakers over time. Sharing is learned and ultimately mastered with time. A preschooler is bound to know a lot more about sharing than the average toddler. Toddlers are instinctively selfish and self-serving. They don't really understand or see the benefit of sharing.

But, much like language and other complex interactional and social practices, sharing is a vital life skill that enables you to create and maintain relationships with people. Sharing unites people and teaches them a little bit about sacrifice, turn-taking, and handling disappointments.

Since sharing is such a vital communicative and survival skill that it is important to monitor your child's growth and interactions. Most children have a hard time sharing, so it's important to teach them about sharing in a fun and non-threatening fashion. The best way to teach your child about sharing is convincing him it was his idea from the start. For example, if you talk about a friend of your child's and how he shared toys in class, your child will be motivated to imitate him. This tactic is especially effective for preschoolers and other kids of school age. You should also practice sharing toys and food with your child and praise him when he manages to get it right. It is important to make him understand when he is doing what is wrong or right. Attitudes and actions must never go unmonitored, especially with kids who are still being introduced to social norms and customs.

Practicing sharing exercises is also a fun way to teach him about turn-taking and momentary dissatisfaction. Momentarily depriving a child of a toy or some form of gratification will allow the child to better handle disappointment and teach him about patience. Although sharing is deeply recommended among growing children, clear boundaries should still be established nonetheless. Certain things should be kept from the sharing exercises. On a fundamental level, every child bonds to items like toys or clothing, and they become inseparable from it. Items like these should not be used in typical sharing exercises.

Not all children typically subscribe to the concept of sharing. They don't just assume it's beneficial or needed. In rare cases like these, we recommend introducing a little bit of punishment to straighten them out. Creating a mild consequence system will help them better adapt and accept the concept of sharing. Each time they fail to share, you can tell them the reason why they are being punished and take away the toy from them for a given period of time. Obviously, you can't punish children who don't share the same way. Toddlers don't perceive sharing the same way preschoolers and school-goers perceive it.

Toddlers think you are punishing them each time you take their toys away. So, whether you are sharing with them or punishing them for it, they will more or less react the same way. Punishing them won't solve anything. They are not empathetic or developed enough to learn anything from punishment.

Pre-schoolers, on the other hand, understand empathize on some level. They understand the concept of fairness and see reason in giving another person an opportunity to enjoy the toy they like. Punishing them by taking away their toy and telling them the reason for the sort of punishment you are implementing will resonate better with pre-schoolers. Even though they are very impatient, they understand cause and effect on some level and are more likely to be corrected by your choice of punishment.

School-goers are more mature and more likely to understand sharing and see the lesson in the punishment that you choose. School goers are easier to reason with and explain concepts to. Their minds are basically sponges and will soak up whatever important sharing lesson you deem important.

Daniel Faber

Letting your toddler play

Watching your child's play is a low impact way of monitoring his progress and making necessary adjustments to his social and intellectual development. Most new parents might not realize this, but it is what they spend most of their time doing when they are not feeding or cleaning up after their kids.

As a parent, you might enjoy keeping your kids under your wing and watching them grow. But, every once in a while, it's better to let them play and discover the world by themselves. The world might be big and scary, but what is really scary is not letting them become self-independent.

Children, by nature, are heavily dependent on their parents. They depend on them for food, entertainment, and even play. Letting your child play without your presence will teach them to latch-off more and explore the world more. In time, they will accept that you will not always be there to help them play and depend on you less for entertainment.

When children play with older partners too frequently, it could stifle their creativity and imagination. When a child has nothing but toys, he has no choice but to come up with elaborate stories and adventures by himself. Adults tend to do most of the imagining in adult-child play sessions. But when play is child-led, their mind goes places and create fascinating characters, beings, and animals.

It helps them build confidence and social independence. Children that are left to themselves to play and develop with time are more likely to have a more conscious sense of self. They will be successful in blending into numerous social situations and confidently interact with people their age with ease.

Self-led play will teach them to soothe themselves and be calmer.

Different cognitive and developmental stages for children

A Swiss developmental psychologist named Jean Piaget posited that there are four distinct cognitive developmental stages in a child. His classification was originally created in 1936, and although a lot has changed since then, his work is still revered and considered to be a standard. Other great psychologists have created an arguably more accurate and all-encompassing division of a child's cognitive growth. The division they put forward accounts for periods that Piaget's classification muddled together. The later classifications, however, don't go into great detail like Piaget's. That is why, we will go over both popular theories.

Piaget's theory attempts to explain the cognitive process of children and to answer the age-old question, "What goes on in a child's mind?" According to his theory, developmental cognition begins when a child is born and lasts up until he is about 15 years old. After then, the child begins to think like an adult, and over the years, he becomes better and better at it. The first stage is the sensorimotor stage, followed by the preoperational, concrete, and formal stages. We already discussed some of these stages of development in chapter one under the developing mind of your toddler. However, the following illustration goes into greater detail and outlines the specific developments that go on in your child's mind. It is worth the re-iteration.

The sensorimotor is the first stage of a child's cognitive development, and it begins when the child is born and lasts up until he is about two years old. In this stage, the child perceives reality by interacting with the environment and other **stimuli**. In this stage, learning is rapid, repetitive, and is primarily achieved through assimilation and accommodation. The child primarily interacts with his environment through his senses. In this stage, it's important that the child defines his realities and establishes a unique self that is unconnected from his environment.

The child also tries to ascribe meaning to objects during this stage. He is not quite there intellectually, and he has to rely on real-life situations and objects to make sense of each of his complex thought processes. This is the stage that children begin to establish relationships with toys and other objects and experience troubles sharing and empathizing. They perceive thoughts and concepts quite literally and they struggle with abstract concepts. The preoperational stage typically lasts for about five years. It lasts from the ages 2-7.

The third stage is the concrete operational stage. It typically lasts from the years 7-11, and during this time, the child begins to create complex thought processes and seek answers to the questions he has always had. They begin to generalize and rely on logic to figure out certain concrete events. They figure out concepts like conversions, and they become more emotionally sufficient and empathetic. At this stage, they still struggle with understanding the abstract. They are still very literal and can only understand solid and concrete things.

The formal operational stage is the last stage in a child's cognitive development. At this stage, they begin to hypothesize and understand the abstract. They begin to think more morally, philosophically, ethically, and politically. They begin to think more deductively and utilize general information to form specific opinions. Essentially, they become mini-adults and form their own theories and opinions on how the world really works.

The second classification focuses less on the cognitive aspect of a child's development and instead, addresses development as a whole. It focuses on the cognitive, behavioral, and physical development of every child and meticulously documents changes over time. The classification divides a child's development into 5 distinct stages. They are Newborn, Infant, Toddler, Preschool, and School-age. The newborn stage lasts for about a month of life. A newborn's responses and movements are mostly automatic. For example, newborns cry when they need something and desire to be held and cared for.

The infant stage starts immediately after the newborn stage and lasts until the end of the first year of life. The new infant stage comes with radical development in skill, bodily control, strength, and mobility. This means your child should start picking things up, crawling around, moving his hands, and sitting without support.

The third stage is the toddler stage. It typically lasts from the ages of 1-3, and during this time, you should notice that your child is walking climbing, jumping, drawing, and even stacking. There is substantial language development during this stage, and your child should be able to communicate using small phrases. It's also during this phase that the kids should be tested for autism or any other condition.

The preschool stage lasts from the ages 3-5 years. This is the stage that most children learn to fine-tune their motor skills. They become more independent and even learn to dress themselves. They also have more bodily strength and can jump, draw, skip, and stand on a single leg for a couple of seconds.

The fifth stage is the school-age stage that lasts for about six years from the ages 6-12. During this period, they become more independent, responsible, confident, and social. They begin to form lasting friendships and begin to develop sexual characteristics and desires.

Nurturing a child is not an easy task. Sometimes you need to take a step back to give them the room to become the person you believe they can be. For kids with autism, the developmental stages are mostly the same. They develop cognitively, physically, and emotionally like the rest of their peers. They only need some help with the social and communicative aspects of development. As parents, it's your job to breach this gap and help them seamlessly integrate into society.

Chapter Nine

YOUR CHILD AND YOUR FAMILY

Autism can do a lot more than ravage your financial reserves and stress your relationship with your spouse or partner. It can affect pretty much everyone in your family in one way or the other. The condition affecting a single member of your family can make you insensitive to the needs of the other members of your family. Suddenly, the other children that need help get little to no help at all. You are inescapably transfixed with the wellbeing of one child, and his sisters and brothers grow up feeling like they matter less or deserve less. If left unchecked, the needs of the children can fester and become a deep loathing that will always cause them to somehow blame you or their brother. In this chapter, we are focusing on how you can prevent that from happening.

We will focus on pain of your other children, your brother, sister, mother, and basically every member of your family. Their needs matter too, and this chapter will ensure that you never forget to look after them while you look after your child.

Taking care of your partner

Some parents don't have partners they can co-parent with. So, if you are among the lucky few who happen to have someone to depend on, you need to realize how blessed you are to not be taking this journey alone.

Whether you are married or not, your spouse is your co-pilot, and they exist in your life to lessen the enormous strain that raising an autistic child can bring. Don't get it wrong, children are a blessing regardless of what condition they are born with, but they can be a handful at times. You need to recognize this and exploit the fact that you have someone who makes your journey a whole lot easier. This means that you have to take time out of your busy schedule to look after their needs too.

Their needs might be emotional or physical. But, as long as it is within your power to do something about it, you should. They could need a personal day, or need a hot meal, or need to talk about your child's condition and the new realities that you both currently share.

As a great partner, you should not limit your attention to clear cries for help. Try to figure out what they need even if they say nothing. You should do things like keep the romance going in your relationship and ask them how they are feeling without them having to ask you. You were adults in a loving relationship before a child came along; there is no reason why that has to change because you have a child with special needs. You need to try to stay true to who you are, no matter what changes.

Taking care of your other children

Your other kids might not let it show, but they need you just as much as their brother or sister with autism does. They might not tell you because they can't express it in words, but ignoring their needs is one of the biggest mistakes you can make. Kids are not as forward-thinking or empathetic as adults are. They will feel neglected and jealous if someone else aside from them is the center of attention all the time.

You need to look after their needs too. It is expected that you will not be able to spend time with them as much as you spend time with your child with special needs, but you can stop jealousy and other types of negative feelings from festering by teaching them all about responsibility and sacrifice.

Explain the concept of autism to them and help them understand why you have to spend so much time looking after their brother or sister. You should also encourage them to talk about it. There are millions of children all over the world with siblings who have autism. Talking about it will show them that they are not as alone as they think, and it will help them come to terms with how different their brothers and sister are.

Spending some one on one time with them without the presence of their sibling is also a great way to look after their needs. Attention is something that can't be replaced with gifts. Organize fun trips or outings with just you guys and try to get to know them outside of the home.

You can also put them in charge of their sibling. In most homes, the brother or sister without the communication disorder is put in charge of the needs of the one who has the condition. This is a fantastic way to help them get accustomed to responsibility and help the sibling bond. Show them the importance of protecting their brother and remind them that you understand and appreciate their sacrifice.

Furthermore, try not to alienate them by trivializing their problems or refusing to see their side of an argument. When arguments break out between siblings, like they normally do, don't just take the side of their autistic sibling. Create a little bit of equality by being unpredictable with your judgments. Whenever they have a problem that seems insignificant, don't ignore them outright. It's important that you acknowledge their pain. It could possibly be a cry for attention.

Ignoring it would make them assume you love them less.

Focusing on every member of your nuclear and extended family

The needs of your grandparents, cousins, uncles, aunts, friends, and other members of your family might not matter as much as the needs of your spouse, your child with ASD, or his brothers and sisters. But, these needs should not be ignored. Family members and friends are like your backup after your means and strength have failed you. If you look after your family and you make them a present part of your life, they can be very impactful and lessen the load of raising your entire family without external support.

If you develop your relationship well enough, they can fill in as potential baby sitters, investors, support groups, or helpers. With their support, your child's life will be filed with friends and helpful family members who love him as much as you do.

The best way to establish a relationship with them is by helping them out when they really need it and supporting them in any way you can. Host family dinners and invite them. Attend social functions that you think are important to them. Talk to them and spend one on one time with them. Treat them as you would your own brother or sister. Never be afraid to talk about your fears and hopes for your child. If you can talk to them about family, then who can you talk to about it?

Chapter Ten

RAISING YOUR CHILD WITH ASD IS JUST LIKE RAISING EVERY OTHER CHILD

It's no secret that raising children with a disability is a difficult task. They are needy, more emotional, and less communicative than other children. With autism, everything is so different. You have to be incredibly sensitive to his wants or needs and try to make sure he doesn't fall behind in his communication.

There are literally hundreds of things you will have to learn and unlearn through the course of raising your child, and that can sometimes feel overwhelming. Many parents may even feel like all they know is a lie, and they are ill-prepared to meet the needs of raising their special needs child fully. Now, we will be discussing how routine and natural it is to raise an autistic child with a solid background in parenting. Much like everything else in life, there is always some degree of carryover. Something you have done before will definitely be easier the second or third time around. Admittedly, the rules have changed a bit, but the basics of nurturing and parenting haven't.

Taking care of them as newborns

Figuring out if your newborn has ASD is difficult. There are no standard tests that can narrow down and identify disruptive behavior in such young children. Although several kinds of research are being carried out all over the world on this specific subject, it will be years before anything substantial ever makes its way into medical science.

It is improbable that you will be able to prove that your child has autism in the first few months of his life. So, as far as you are concerned, he is just a cute regular baby that needs intense care. The parenting process is still relatively normal at this point and it will remain that way until the child gets tested a few months down the line.

During the newborn months and early months of infancy, you will need all the help you can get. This means relying on friends and families to take the load off every once in a while and taking the occasional break. Everything you learned the first time around still applies. And if you're a new parent who is scared of autism, it is recommended that you wait and hear definite news before panicking. If you are new to parenting and you have no idea how to care for a newborn, here are some things you should watch out for.

Newborns are fragile in every sense of the word. This means that everything from their bones to their immune system is still in development and is still very weak. You need to take special care when you are holding them, and it is recommended that you keep a hand sanitizer handy throughout the early days of maturity.

Also, holding your newborn the right way is one of the basics of early parenthood. It's fairly simple and straightforward. You should always try to support both his head and body while you hold him at all times. Like we mentioned earlier, they are still very fragile and cannot support any part of their bodies, including their own heads.

You should also learn about basics of childcare, which includes how to change a diaper properly, playing with your newborn, swaddling, feeding, and sleeping.

There are numerous videos online teaching new parents how to take care of their newborns. There is a vast wealth of resources in the form of books, videos, and free support groups. If you pay close attention to the wealth of information currently available, it will be incredibly difficult to mess up as a parent.

Raising an infant

In some rare cases, infants are diagnosed within the first six to twelve months of their lives. This is mostly due to overtly disruptive behavior, and at such a tender age, the additional needs are not substantial enough to completely disrupt your life. Granted, it is often said that early intervention is the best help for children with autism. But, there is such a thing as too early. In most cases, if an infant has shown signs of early onset of autism, he is placed in a program designed to speed up his development and potentially have him ready for kindergarten. Unfortunately, most of those treatment plans and courses are designed for children who are above the ages of 1 year. This means that you could help your child if you really wanted, but if you discover autism too early, there is really nothing that can be done about it for the meantime.

When a baby hits the six months threshold, it's time to mix up their diet a little bit. You don't have to completely wean them off breast milk; you just have to introduce semi-solids into their diets and feed them with plates and spoons. You should also have them eating while sitting up, and massage their aching gums every day or so.

You will also need to stop moving them in walkers. This will prevent falls and injuries.

Taking care of your toddler and preschooler

This is the stage in a baby's development when actual communication begins to happen. He starts to talk, and it is at this age that you can look into ways of helping him learn the language and social communication more automatically. At that tender age, their minds are basically sponges that soak up information. During this time, you should visit multiple doctors, psychologists, and therapists. This is the time that some of the behavioral issues will set in. Admittedly, it's very different from what most parents are used to, but if you analyze it slowly and more meticulously, you'll find out that it's not so different from what you would typically do if you had a toddler or preschooler his age.

Every preschooler or toddler is unique in his own way. If you've ever had a baby, you'll notice that he is completely different from his other brothers and sisters. Each toddler is like a little snowflake in a vast sea of fresh snow. They pick up on things at a different pace, they like different things, and above everything else, and they have different strength and weaknesses. Regardless of whether your child has autism or not, you will have that to look forward to. You should also know that the behavioral changes you see at this age might not be even related to ASD. It might just be a child growing up and being a snowflake.

Toddlers are incredibly energetic and wild. They look small and cute, but they leave the biggest mess. ou should never misconstrue your child's hyperactivity as a sure sign of autism. While autistic children have been known to be quite the nightmare, seemingly limitless energy is not a feature that is exclusive to only those types of children. You'll still have to clean up a million stains, spills and vomits while your little one is still a toddler, that remains the same regardless of whether your child is autistic or not.

A big part of raising a child with autism is setting a routine, but so is raising a toddler. Whether you are the parent to an autistic child or not, you will always have to plan your day and come up with a routine to manage your toddler's disruptive behavior. You have to think about things like feeding behavior, hyperactivity, and tantrums. There is no getting around these three things. Children cry, scream, and create episodes when they are scared or alone or upset. Kids with ASD might get upset more frequently and make more scenes, but this isn't an agreed-upon fact. When you don't look after the needs of your child, they will get upset. A child being autistic does not automatically mean he will be more difficult to deal with.

You will be surprised how difficult certain kids can be.

Kids, in general, are more observant than adults give them credit for. If you fight constantly with your spouse or you curse, the odds are that your kids are listening to you and will most likely imitate you eventually. Unfortunaely, while you willingly admit whenever you mess up, they are free-spirited and unapologetic. You can expect episodes explaining your bad behavior whether your child has autism or not.

Raising a school goer or teenager

Raising your teenager or school goer is a lot more complicated than raising a toddler. When a child enters his preteen and teens, he begins to perceive the world more logically. He gets the ability to form his own views and will begin to distance himself from you. They will want their independence, and it will be your job to slowly give it to them as they mature.

They will also be curious about their sexuality. When children are in their preteens, they begin to see the sexual side of most relationships they share with their peers. When this happens, you will most likely have to talk about sex and teach them about safe sex and the advantage of waiting.

This discussion is undoubtedly harder with kids with autism, but it's not as different as you would think. Depending on how close you are with them, your preteen will either come to you for answers about sexuality or they will turn to another person they trust. They might have trouble talking about how they feel and figuring out the nature of their relationship with certain people. This might, in some cases, cause them to make unhealthy decisions that might affect them emotionally. You will also have to desensitize them and help them better deal with their sensory issues.

This sometimes means helping them overcome some of their sensory issues. Although some of the issues raised are exclusive to kids with autism, most are universal and affect kids regardless of their communicative and social skills. All teenagers feel clueless when it comes to navigating relationships. They can sometimes get confused, make bad decisions, or have problems expressing their emotions. It is your job as a great parent to give great sex education to all your kids and give them enough information to make the right decision at every turn.

Sex might be a major part of raising a teenager or preteen, but it's not all there is to bringing up an upstanding member of society. At every point in a teen's life, he formulates certain ideologies about what he believes in. It might be ideological, moral, religious, or even philosophical. They will turn to you sooner or later for some kind of input. For most kids, it's a talk about morals, ideologies, and belief systems. With kids with autism however, it's a little bit more complicated than that. They may want to understand the logic behind certain structures. It will be your job to break down challenging concepts like moral ambiguity, altruism, and self-love to them. These talks are sometimes more challenging, but they are not totally different from what you would expect from a child without autism.

Every child goes through a rebellious phase. Dealing with your child's rebellious spell in your own unique way is a necessary and often crucial part of bringing up your son or daughter. Understanding their pains and motivation is vital, and it is usually the first step of curbing their disruptive behavior. Kids, irrespective of their communicative or social strengths, are prone to overt displays of aggression. This is usually caused by some inner desire to find themselves or seek attention. The cry for help might be buried under an obscene layer of teenage angst and anger, but it is, in most cases, the cause of their worrisome behavior. When this happens, punishment and profound healing sessions are habitually part of the rehabilitation process. Parents will often talk to their children and try to focus less on the how, and more on the why.

With children with autism, the process is incredibly similar. The sort of punishment administered and the things you talk about might be different, but the structure remains the same. Your teenage son might choose to cause trouble at school because he feels like you're not spending enough time with him. If he is autistic, you will probably try to figure out if he recognizes how bad what he did was. If he knows what he did was bad, the next step would be to come up with suitable punishment and finally find out the root of the problem. If he does not know what he did was bad, it would be your job to tell him why by using social concepts like empathy. It can be said that disciplining your autistic child might a bit more challenging, but it was built on the foundations laid down by everyday parents.

The notion that autistic children require a different blueprint or manual altogether is an inaccurate description of what parenting an autistic child is really like. There is a huge disconnect between what is portrayed by the media and what actually happens when you raise an autistic child. Too many generalizations happen, and not enough fact-driven information makes it to mass media. Hopefull, this chapter has succeeded in clearing up the widespread misconceptions and half-truths by talking about what really goes on during the parenting process.

Chapter Eleven

CAN PEOPLE WITH AUTISM LEAD A NORMAL LIFE?

As we are almost at the end of this book, your brain is no doubt swirling with all this new information. You're probably conflicted about how to feel and are torn between excitement and anxiety. On the one hand, you've gained a wealth of knowledge about how to care for your autistic child. On the other hand, you now know so much more about the condition, and that can be scary. One question that will be on your mind, above all else, is whether or not people with autism can lead a normal life.

As a parent, it's only natural for you to want to care for your child. You want him to have the best possible life, and his autism is making you question whether or not that's possible. We will close this book with some good news. It is possible for people with ASD to lead a normal life. However, it all depends on what you describe as normal.

You have to understand that you can't describe normal in the same terms as someone who doesn't have ASD. In fact, your child may never be able to fully comprehend how other people live their lives. And he shouldn't. Because as long as you're happy in this life, nothing else should matter. There are people who received the diagnosis at young as 3 years, and they've lived to be 70 years old. They have led full, productive lives and have lived as good members of the society. So while it's certainly normal to worry about the wellbeing of your child, your worry and anxiety might be a little misplaced.

The communications training and treatment plans that you have incorporated into your child's life aim to make his life much easier. You teach him communication to enable him to communicate better with everyone around him. You teach emotional control because he needs to be able to handle adversity. Even the concept of the schedule is designed to make his entire life more structured. In essence, you've been training your child to be normal since the day you found out about the diagnosis. You should take comfort in this knowledge and understand that you've done all you can to make his life better.

What does being on the two extreme ends of the spectrum mean for your kid when he is an adult?

Autism Spectrum Disorders typically range from the mild to the extreme, or settle somewhere in between. Up until recently, the various types and degrees of communicative, social and behavioral disorders were given different terms.

The milder, more manageable end of the spectrum was referred to as Asperger's syndrome, and the more pervasive and severe type of communicative disability was called Childhood disintegrative disorder. Both these extremes affect children differently, and it is sometimes surprising how different children with types of ASD can be. In between those two extremes, you have the Pervasive developmental disorder popularly referred to as PDD, the eponymous autistic disorder, and the rare Rett Syndrome, which is technically not ASD since it is caused by a genetic mutation.

Belonging on alternating sides of the spectrum can be a good or bad thing for your child while transitioning to adulthood. While, it is entirely possible for him to lead a full life, he will need a couple of years to catch up. He will need time to become accustomed to dealing with people and overcoming all sorts of communicative limitations.

The number of years he remain entirely dependent on you, will vary depending on the area of the autism scale he belongs to. In some cases, independent living might be simply impossible for some children. Their symptoms are simply more advanced than others, and they might never truly become fully autonomous. They can, however, become semi-autonomous and function actively with the help of a caretaker.

Asperger's syndrome and functioning independently

Children who are diagnosed with Asperger's Syndrome are more limited socially. This means that while they thrive in arithmetic, problem solving and basically every other aspect of his daily live, they still have problems functioning socially. They will have a hard time starting and maintaining all sorts of social and emotional relationships.

Your child's communicative and social competence will improve eventually, but it won't happen overnight. This means that up until he is halfway through his mid-twenties, he will need some level of supervision. By supervision, we don't mean continuing your job as the overprotective mother or father, we mean requesting some type of care giver, usually low impact, from the state when he first moves away from you.

If your child decides to go off to college, he will be about nineteen years old when he starts in as a freshman. Most nineteen years old freshmen don't have any control over their lives, and your child with ASD is no different. He will need some supervision, and he will most likely live with a couple of other autistic kid and will be catered for by an employee of the state. He will get help when he needs it, and will eventually, when the time comes, age out, and go out into the world and become a functional member of society.

During his time with the government-hired caretaker, he will be taught to find and keep a job. This process will be no doubt tedious, but it will be worth it. He will learnt to adapt, be comfortable, and be productive without getting agitated by slight inconveniences.

After he leaves college, and no longer has access to a government paid caregiver, he will have a lot of growing up to do in a relatively short amount of time. This means that he will have to live without some form of supervision for the first time in his life. This change can be very scary, and he will most likely, not be ready for it. What we recommend is talking him into living with another person with ASD, or living with someone in general. This way, he is living with someone who can help if he should need it, and he has some degree of true independence.

Childhood disintegrative disorder and functioning independently

Childhood disintegrative disorder is the rarest and most severe type of autism disorder. Children with this type of ASD, need more care and attention than most. Children with Childhood disintegrative disorder lose most of their social, language and sometimes mental skills between from the ages of three. This means that everything they have learnt up until that point will slowly erode away. This type of ASD is characterized by seizures, loss of mobility, loss of language skills, inability to express communicative needs, loss of hand-eye coordination, etc.

CDD is no doubt every parent's nightmare, but it's doesn't have to mean the end for your child. The progression of CDD varies from child to child, and early intervention always makes a difference. With enough therapy, support and attention, your child can relearn some of his lost fundamental communicative, social, mental, and motor skills. There is no guarantee he will be as independent as other kids on the milder side of the spectrum, but he could still attain some level of control and autonomy. With a full time caregiver, who has been professionally trained, he can thrive and function without you necessarily being around all the time.

Autistic Disorder and functioning independently

By autism disorder, we are not referring to the spectrum per se, we are talking about the isolated disorder that is characterized by repetitive behavior and slow social development. It is a lot like the Asperger's disorder, only it is more severe.

This disorder is a lot like the Asperger's disorder in more ways than one. Children with this kind of disorder too can function independently at some points in their lives. Like with the Asperger's disorder, it might take a lot of time and attention, but it will happen eventually. The only problem with this kind of disorder is that it leaves a lot of wiggle room. The symptoms could range from very mild to very serious. This means that factors like early intervention, great therapy, and an enabling environment will go a long way to alleviate the problems that usually develop earlier on.

Your child might stay dependent on you for a bit longer than you expect, and he might need a little more support, but eventually, he will be able to go out on his own, and become his own person. This means that you will have to find a caretaker in the meantime, and help him get him used to the challenges of adulthood.

Pervasive developmental disorder and living independently

Pervasive development disorder is a technical term used to refer to people on the autism spectrum whose symptoms are somewhere between Asperger's disorder and the autism disorder. This disorder is typically characterized by difficulty using language, difficulty interacting with people objects, and events, difficultly managing change, spontaneous and repetitive movements, emotional episodes, and a lot of other unique quirks. The most notable of all these symptoms is the communicative peculiarities that sometimes involves lack of eye contact, pointing behaviors and difficulty using facial expressions.

This kind of autism is right down in the middle of the spectrum, and can often times be very tricky to handle. As we have mentioned numerous times, therapy and early intervention makes all the difference. PDD often occurs in degrees, and some children experience more serious symptoms than others. Some children with PDD could have a relatively decent mastery over language, and others won't be able to speak at all. This inconsistency, as you might have noticed, can be found across the spectrum. So, the kind or level of independence your child eventually attains throughout his life is heavily dependent on the severity of his symptoms.

With mild symptoms, he could possibly go to some college or vocational institute of his choosing, and eventually learn to become moderately independent. He might have to live with roommates all his life, but he will attain some level of independence. On the other hand, if he his symptoms are more severe, he will need more support and attention. He will constantly need some form of communicative aid like sign language. Regardless of the effects his symptoms, he should still be able to leave home eventually.

Letting go

It is admittedly difficult to watch your beautiful little chick spread his wings and leave the nest. As parents, you have to understand that your child with ASD will need to explore and become a person outside the guidelines that you have set up for him.

When your kid decides to go off to college or choose some kind of vocation or training of some kind, this is usually a sign that he thinks he is ready to begin his journey by himself. While, it's your job as his parents to fight him every step of the way, you have to recognize the importance of letting him function and thrive outside our purview or protection.

Dealing with the state cutting you off

We mentioned at an earlier chapter that some states in America and Europe provide some level of financial aid for children with autism. That often expires when your child is about twenty one years old. The support checks will halt at this point, and it will be up to you to provide all the care from that point onwards. Children with ASD need supervision until they are about twenty five years at least. That is four whole years that the government won't be helping your with the bills. As responsible parents, you must identify and plan for this development well beforehand.

No established insurance plan has coverage extensive to cover the medical and living expenses of your child, so what we recommend is cutting down on cost without necessarily reducing attention and care. This is where the group home or roommate idea comes into play. With the group home or roommate idea, your child and bunch of other children with ASD live together in an apartment together. Between the kids and their parents, they will be able to pull enough resources for a caretaker, and help will always be at the ready when the kids need it.

The Verdict

At the end of it all, autism is a permanent neurological deficit, and all you can do is manage it. But with the variety of treatment options available today, people with autism can lead long and very productive lives. It may not be the same as people without ASD, but it is much better than you would ever imagine it to be.

CONCLUSION

It must have been quite an experience reading this book. Receiving all this new information is going to be jarring for anyone. Learning that your child has Autism is something that most parents never really recover from. Even though you love your child, it's impossible to resist wishing things were different. Unfortunately, they are not and you're going to have to live with the condition.

Just like we've discussed over and over in this book, you have to understand that it's all about your child at this point. You may have to raise him, but he's going to have to learn to grow, live, and thrive with the condition. As we discussed in the last chapter, people with ASD can live full and productive lives, so you don't have to be concerned about looking after him for the rest of his life. He'll figure it out eventually. Even though it's a condition that most people want nothing to do with, it's not the end of the world. In fact, it's a new beginning.

Take this book as a guide for when you feel stuck and confused about the best way to proceed with your child's care. While it's not a book on parenting per se, it contains invaluable information on raising and befriending your child. As you've already learned, parenting is not the easiest job in the world. Raising a child with autism is even more challenging.

It all begins with understanding that after all is said and done, your child is still a child. He has mental and psychological developmental milestones that he must reach, just like every other child. He does things that you can't quite explain, throws tantrums, refrains from sharing, and puts everything in his mouth, just like every other child.

The only difference is that your child might achieve these developmental milestones slower than other children, and that's where your love and attention come in. Your child will also need special help interacting with other children because his social skills won't come as easily. YOU may have to engage tactics like role-playing, explaining, and teaching him how to learn to lose.

As we've explained throughout the book, parenting a child with autism is like parenting 2.0. You'll need all the lessons you've from parenting your non-autistic children, plus some new ones. Learning how to communicate, structuring your days, and coping with stress are on the top of the list. You'll also need to learn how to create an environment where your child can thrive while also finding creative and practical ways to solve everyday problems.

While this book is not a complete guide on parenting, it will give you invaluable information when you're trying to parent your autistic child. Like most parents, you'll realize that it doesn't necessarily get easier. You just get better at it. You can also relax knowing the fact that no matter your child's position on the autism spectrum, he can have a very long and fulfilling life. And that in itself is rewarding enough.

Printed in Great Britain
by Amazon